White

Seeing White All around Us

by Michael Dahl

Consulting Editor: Gail Saunders-Smith, PhD

Capstone
press

Mankato, Minnesota

A+ Books are published by Capstone Press,
151 Good Counsel Drive, P.O. Box 669, Mankato, Minnesota 56002.
www.capstonepress.com

1 2 3 4 5 6 10 09 08 07 06 05

Library of Congress Cataloging-in-Publication Data
Dahl, Michael.
  White: seeing white all around us / by Michael Dahl.
    p. cm.—(A+ Books. Colors)
  Includes bibliographical references and index.
  ISBN-13: 978-0-7368-3671-5 (hardcover)   ISBN-10: 0-7368-3671-3 (hardcover)
  ISBN-13: 978-0-7368-5073-5 (softcover pbk.)   ISBN-10: 0-7368-5073-2 (softcover pbk.)
  1. White—Juvenile literature. 2. Color—Juvenile literature. I. Title. II. Series.
QC495.5.D348 2005
535.6—dc22   2004014353

Summary: Text and photographs describe common things that are white, including teeth, polar bears, and baseballs.

Credits
Blake A. Hoena, editor; Heather Kindseth, designer; Kelly Garvin, photo researcher

Photo Credits
Ardea/M. Watson, 18–19
Capstone Press/Gary Sundermeyer, cover, 28, 29 (all)
Capstone Press/Karon Dubke, 3 (all), 4–5, 6–7, 8–9, 10–11, 12–13, 14–15, 16–17, 20, 24–25, 32 (all)
Corbis/Japack Company, 22–23
SuperStock/Yoshio Tomii, 26–27

Note to Parents, Teachers, and Librarians
The Colors books use full-color photographs and a nonfiction format to introduce children to the world of color. *White* is designed to be read aloud to a pre-reader or to be read independently by an early reader. Photographs and activities help listeners and early readers understand the text and concepts discussed. The book encourages further learning by including the following sections: Table of Contents, Glossary, Read More, Internet Sites, and Index. Early readers may need assistance using these features.

Table of Contents

White is something that you wear.

The fastest sailboats can race through the water at more than 50 miles an hour.

White can catch a gust of air.

A hen lays an average of five eggs per week. That equals 260 eggs a year.

White gets scrambled.
White gets fried.

Whipped cream is just what its name says. Cream is whipped until it becomes foamy and full of tiny air bubbles.

White can sit on top of pies.

11

Adults have more teeth than children. Adults have 32 teeth, and children have 20.

White can chew, and white can bite.

White can hold
the words you write.

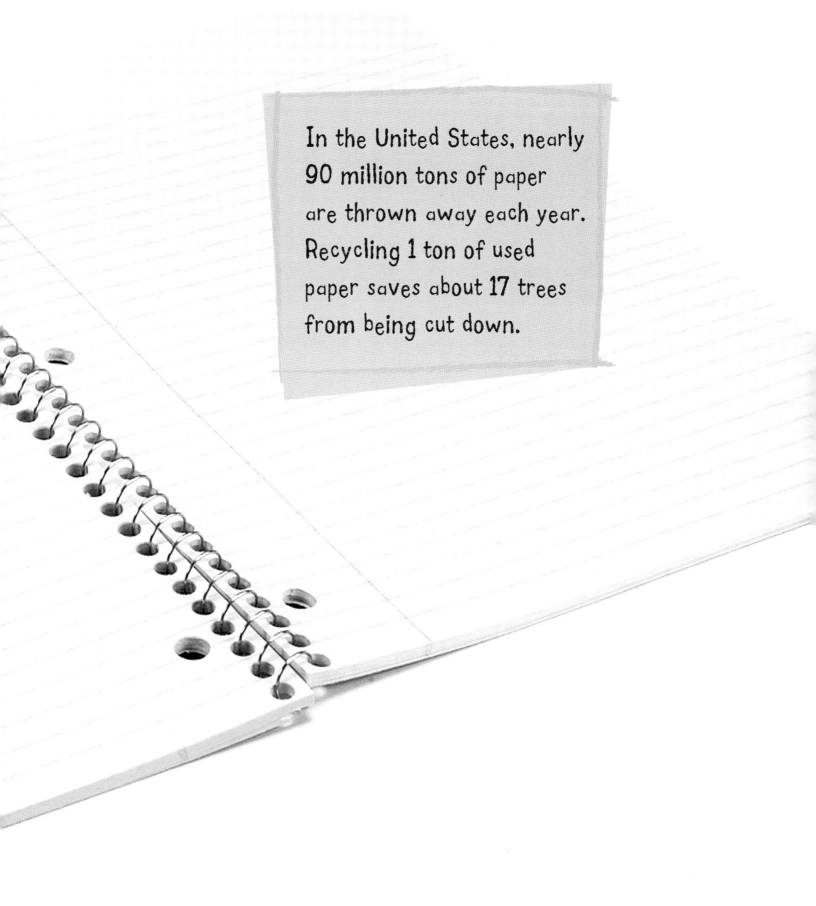

In the United States, nearly 90 million tons of paper are thrown away each year. Recycling 1 ton of used paper saves about 17 trees from being cut down.

Elmer's is a brand name of glue. It was named after a cartoon character called Elmer the Bull. Elmer is married to Elsie the Cow, the spokescow for the white stuff on page 20.

White can stick things together.

White lives
in snowy weather.

Do you have hair on the bottom of your feet? A polar bear does. The hair on its paws keeps it from slipping and sliding on ice.

A dairy cow makes about 200,000 glasses of milk in her lifetime. That's enough milk to fill an average-sized swimming pool.

White can fill up your glass.

Wind spreads dandelion seeds. The feathery part of a seed acts like a parachute. It catches the wind and helps the seed float through the air.

White floats
above the grass.

Early baseballs were made from whatever people could find. Some baseballs were made by winding string around a walnut or by wrapping a rock in cloth.

White gets smacked with a bat.

White can wear
a scarf and hat.

Making Tints of Colors

Artists use white to make colors lighter. A lighter hue of a color is called a tint.

You will need

paint tray

white paint

yellow paint

blue paint

paintbrushes

colored paper

1 Put white paint in the middle of the paint tray. Add yellow and blue around the white.

2 Using a paintbrush, move some of the yellow paint to a clean spot on the paint tray. Then add a small amount of white to the new portion of yellow. Mix the colors together. Notice that the yellow gets lighter. Using a clean paintbrush, repeat this step with the blue paint.

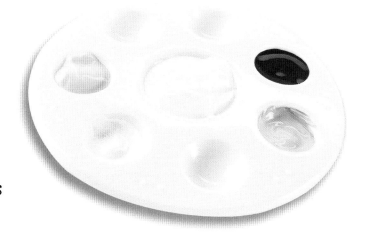

3 To make the tints of yellow and blue lighter, add small amounts of white. When you're finished mixing, use the colors to paint your masterpiece.

Glossary

fry (FRYE)—to cook food in hot oil

gust (GUHST)—a sudden, strong blast of wind

hen (HEN)—a female chicken

hue (HYOO)—a color or variation of a color

parachute (PAR-uh-shoot)—a large piece of fabric that lets people safely drop from airplanes

recycle (ree-SYE-kuhl)—to use old items, such as tires, aluminum cans, and newspapers, to make new items

scramble (SKRAM-buhl)—to mix together and cook

tint (TINT)—a lighter hue of a color

whip (WIP)—to beat something, such as cream or eggs, until it becomes foamy

Read More

Parker, Victoria. *White with Other Colors.* Mixing Colors. Chicago: Raintree, 2004.

Whitehouse, Patricia. *White Foods.* The Colors We Eat. Chicago: Heinemann Library, 2002.

Winne, Joanne. *White in My World.* The World of Color. New York: Children's Press, 2000.

Internet Sites

FactHound offers a safe, fun way to find Internet sites related to this book. All of the sites on FactHound have been researched by our staff.

Here's how:

1. Visit *www.facthound.com*
2. Type in this special code **0736836713** for age-appropriate sites. Or enter a search word related to this book for a more general search.
3. Click on the **Fetch It** button.

FactHound will fetch the best sites for you!

Index